Post your finished work and join the community.
#FAITHINCOLOR

O HOLY NIGHT
ADULT COLORING BOOK
COLOR and Contemplate the Reason for the Season

PASSIO

O, Holy Night

O, holy night, the stars are brightly shining;
It is the night of the dear Savior's birth!
Long lay the world in sin and error pining,
Till He appeared and the soul felt its worth.
A thrill of hope, the weary soul rejoices,
For yonder breaks a new and glorious morn.

Fall on your knees, O, hear the angel voices!
O, night divine, O, night when Christ was born!
O, night divine, O, night, O, night divine!

Led by the light of faith serenely beaming,
With glowing hearts by His cradle we stand.
So led by light of a star sweetly gleaming,
Here came the wise men from Orient land.
The King of kings lay thus in lowly manger,
In all our trials born to be our Friend!

He knows our need—to our weakness is no stranger.
Behold your King; before Him lowly bend!
Behold your King; before Him lowly bend!

Truly He taught us to love one another;
His law is love and His Gospel is peace.
Chains shall He break for the slave is our brother,
And in His Name all oppression shall cease.
Sweet hymns of joy in grateful chorus raise we,
Let all within us praise His holy Name!

Christ is the Lord! O, praise His name forever!
His pow'r and glory evermore proclaim!
His pow'r and glory evermore proclaim!

—Placide Cappeau

In the Beginning...

Our eternal salvation began with our Savior's birth. Inspired by one of the most beloved songs describing this life-altering event, "O Holy Night," the richly detailed designs in this adult coloring book will help relieve your stress as they provide calmness and serenity in the midst of the busyness of the Christmas season. As you color, reflect on that momentous birth and remember that it was God's amazing love for you that compelled Him to send His only Son to earth so you could have eternal life.

Novices and experienced colorists alike will be able to reflect upon short quotations from the Modern English Version of the Bible as they color the rich tapestry of holiday motifs on every page. The Modern English Version (MEV) is the most modern translation produced in the King James tradition within the last thirty years. This formal equivalence translation maintains the beauty of the past yet provides fresh clarity for a new generation of Bible readers. If you would like more information on the MEV, please visit www.mevbible.com.

In addition to the short quotations throughout this book, you might enjoy reading the Christmas story from the Gospel of Matthew. We hope this passage inspires you to make the most of the Christmas season. As you color, remember that the best artistic endeavors have no rules. Unleash your creativity as you experiment with colors, textures, and mediums. Freedom of self-expression will help to release wellness, balance, mindfulness, and inner peace into your life, allowing you to enjoy the process as well as the finished product. When you're finished, you can frame your favorite creations for displaying or gift giving. Then post your artwork on Facebook, Twitter, or Instagram with the hashtag #FAITHINCOLOR.

The Birth of Jesus

Now the birth of Jesus Christ happened this way: After His mother Mary was engaged to Joseph, before they came together, she was found with child by the Holy Spirit. Then Joseph her husband, being a just man and not willing to make her a public example, had in mind to divorce her privately.

But while he thought on these things, the angel of the Lord appeared to him in a dream saying, "Joseph, son of David, do not be afraid to take Mary as your wife, for He who is conceived in her is of the Holy Spirit. She will bear a Son, and you shall call His name JESUS, for He will save His people from their sins."

Now all this occurred to fulfill what the Lord had spoken through the prophet, saying, "A virgin shall be with child, and will bear a Son, and they shall call His name Immanuel," which is interpreted, "God with us."

Then Joseph, being awakened from sleep, did as the angel of the Lord had commanded him, and remained with his wife, and did not know her until she had given birth to her firstborn Son. And he called His name JESUS.

—MATTHEW 1:18–25, MEV

For God so loved the world that He gave His only begotten Son, that whoever believes in Him should not perish, but have eternal life. For God did not send His Son into the world to condemn the world, but that the world through Him might be saved.

—J OHN 3:16–17, MEV

For unto us a child is born, unto us a son is given.

—I<small>SAIAH</small> 9:6<small>A</small>, MEV

And this is the testimony: that God has given us

eternal life, and this life is in His Son.

—1 JOHN 5:11, MEV

GOD has given us ETERNAL LIFE and this LIFE is in His SON

—1 JOHN 5:11

Rejoice greatly, O daughter of Zion! And cry aloud, O daughter of Jerusalem! See, your king is coming to you; he is righteous and able to deliver.

—ZECHARIAH 9:9A, MEV

When they saw the star, they rejoiced with great excitement.

—Matthew 2:10, MEV

In the beginning was the Word, and the Word was with God, and the Word was God. He was in the beginning with God. All things were created through Him, and without Him nothing was created that was created. In Him was life, and the life was the light of mankind. The light shines in darkness, but the darkness has not overcome it.

—JOHN 1:1–5, MEV

In Him was Life, AND THE Life was the Light of Mankind. John 1:4

And then an angel of the Lord appeared to them, and

the glory of the Lord shone around them.

—Luke 2:9a, MEV

But when the fullness of time came, God sent forth His

Son, born from a woman…to redeem those who were under

the law, that we might receive the adoption as sons.

—GALATIANS 4:4–5, MEV

The angel of the Lord appeared to him in a dream saying, "Joseph, son of David, do not be afraid to take Mary as your wife, for He who is conceived in her is of the Holy Spirit."

—Matthew 1:20, mev

He will be great, and will be called the Son of the Highest.

And the Lord God will give Him the throne of His father

David, and He will reign over the house of Jacob forever.

And of His kingdom there will be no end.

—Luke 1:32–33, mev

Look, the Lamb of God, who takes away the sin of the world.

—JOHN 1:29B, MEV

And when they came into the house, they saw the young Child

with Mary, His mother, and fell down and worshipped Him.

—MATTHEW 2:11A, MEV

They saw the young Child with Mary, His mother, and fell down and worshipped Him.

—MATTHEW 2:11A

This is a faithful saying and worthy of all acceptance, that Christ Jesus came into the world to save sinners, of whom I am the worst. But I received mercy for this reason, that in me, first, Jesus Christ might show all patience, as an example to those who were to believe in Him for eternal life. Now to the eternal, immortal, invisible King, the only wise God, be honor and glory forever. Amen.

—1 TIMOTHY 1:15–17, MEV

Christ Jesus came into the World to save sinners

1 Timothy 1:15

And the star which they saw in the east went before them

until it came and stood over where the young Child was.

—Matthew 2:9b, MEV

And his name shall be called Wonderful Counselor,

Mighty God, Eternal Father, Prince of Peace.

—Isaiah 9:6b, MEV

But the angel said to them, "Listen! Do not fear. For I bring

you good news of great joy, which will be to all people."

—LUKE 2:10, MEV

A star will come out of Jacob,

and a scepter will rise out of Israel.

—NUMBERS 24:17B, MEV

And Mary said: "My soul magnifies the Lord, and my

spirit rejoices in God my Savior."

—LUKE 1:46–47, MEV

God my Savior

LUKE 1:47

And we have seen and testify that the Father sent the

Son to be the Savior of the world.

—1 John 4:14, MEV

Therefore the Lord Himself shall give you a sign: The virgin shall

conceive, and bear a son, and shall call his name Immanuel.

—Isaiah 7:14, MEV

And she gave birth to her firstborn Son, and wrapped

Him in strips of cloth, and laid Him in a manger,

because there was no room for them in the inn.

—LUKE 2:7, MEV

So they came hurrying and found Mary and Joseph,

and the Baby lying in a manger.

—LUKE 2:16, MEV

But the angel said to her, "Do not be afraid, Mary,

for you have found favor with God."

—L*UKE* 1:30, MEV

She will bear a Son, and you shall call His name

JESUS, for He will save His people from their sins.

—MATTHEW 1:21, MEV

And there shall come forth a shoot from the stump of

Jesse, and a Branch shall grow out of his roots.

—Isaiah 11:1, MEV

Now after Jesus was born in Bethlehem of Judea in the days of Herod the king, wise men came from the east to Jerusalem, saying, "Where is He who was born King of the Jews? For we have seen His star in the east and have come to worship Him."

—MATTHEW 2:1–2, MEV

And in the same area there were shepherds living in

the fields, keeping watch over their flock by night.

—LUKE 2:8, MEV

Of the increase of his government

and peace there shall be no end.

—I<small>SAIAH</small> 9:7<small>A</small>, <small>MEV</small>

Jesus answered, "You say correctly that I am a king.

For this reason I was born, and for this reason I came

into the world, to bear witness to the truth. Everyone

who is of the truth hears My voice."

—JOHN 18:37B, MEV

Again, Jesus spoke to them, saying "I am the light of the world. Whoever follows Me shall not walk in the darkness, but shall have the light of life."

—JOHN 8:12, MEV

Glory to God in the highest, and on earth peace,

and good will toward men.

—Luke 2:14, MEV

For my eyes have seen Your salvation which You have

prepared in the sight of all people, a light for revelation to

the Gentiles, and the glory of Your people Israel.

—LUKE *2:30–32,* MEV

The angel answered her, "The Holy Spirit will come upon you, and the power of the Highest will overshadow you. Therefore the Holy One who will be born will be called the Son of God."

—LUKE 1:35, MEV

The Word became flesh and dwelt among us,

and we saw His glory, the glory as the only

Son of the Father, full of grace and truth.

—JOHN 1:14, MEV

And He will reign over the house of Jacob forever. And

of His kingdom there will be no end.

—L*UKE* 1:33, MEV

AND OF *His* Kingdom THERE WILL BE *no end.*

—LUKE 1:33

And you, Bethlehem, in the land of Judah, are no longer

least among the princes of Judah; for out of you shall

come a Governor, who will shepherd My people Israel.

—MATTHEW 2:6, MEV

Listen, you will conceive in your womb and bear

a Son and shall call His name JESUS.

—LUKE 1:31, MEV

And when they had opened their treasures, they

presented gifts to Him: gold, frankincense, and myrrh.

—MATTHEW 2:11B, MEV

Every good gift and every perfect gift is from above

and comes down from the Father of lights, with whom

is no change or shadow of turning.

—JAMES 1:17, MEV

And this will be a sign to you: You will find the Baby

wrapped in strips of cloth, lying in a manger.

—LUKE 2:12, MEV

For unto you is born this day in the City of David

a Savior, who is Christ the Lord.

—*Luke 2:11, MEV*

"A virgin shall be with child, and will bear a Son, and they shall call His name Immanuel," which is interpreted, "God with us."

—MATTHEW 1:23, MEV

For the wages of sin is death, but the gift of God

is eternal life through Jesus Christ our Lord.

—Romans 6:23, MEV

But when the kindness and the love of God our Savior toward

mankind appeared, not by works of righteousness which we

have done, but according to His mercy He saved us, through the

washing of rebirth and the renewal of the Holy Spirit, whom He

poured out on us abundantly through Jesus Christ our Savior, so

that, being justified by His grace, we might become heirs

according to the hope of eternal life.

—TITUS 3:4–7, MEV

My sheep hear My voice, and I know them, and they follow

Me. I give them eternal life. They shall never perish, nor

shall anyone snatch them from My hand.

—JOHN 10:27–28, MEV

May all kings bow down before him; may all nations serve him.

—PSALM 72:11, MEV

Most CHARISMA HOUSE BOOK GROUP products are available at
special quantity discounts for bulk purchase for sales promotions,
premiums, fund-raising, and educational needs. For details, write
Charisma House Book Group, 600 Rinehart Road, Lake Mary,
Florida 32746, or telephone (407) 333-0600.

O HOLY NIGHT published by Passio
Charisma Media/Charisma House Book Group
600 Rinehart Road
Lake Mary, Florida 32746
www.charismahouse.com

Design Director: Justin Evans
Cover Design: Justin Evans
Interior Design: Justin Evans, Lisa Rae McClure, Vincent Pirozzi

Illustrations: Getty Images / Depositphotos

International Standard Book Number: 978-1-62998-909-9

This publication is translated in Spanish under the title *Santa la
noche*, copyright © 2016, published by Casa Creación, a Charisma
Media company. All rights reserved.

First edition

16 17 18 19 20 — 987654321

Printed in the United States of America